Table of Contents

Rourke
Educational Media
rourkeeducationalmedia.com

Can you find these words?

Declaration

events

independence

visit

A symbol stands for an idea.

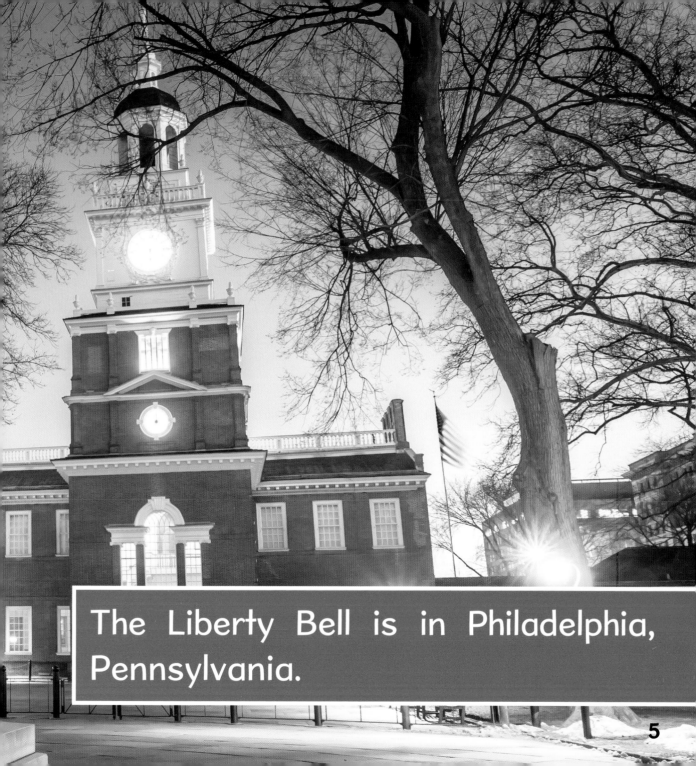

The Liberty Bell is in Philadelphia, Pennsylvania.

It is a symbol of freedom. It is a symbol of **independence.**

e World's Symbol for Liberty

Ring, ring! The bell brought people to listen.

THE FOURTH OF JULY AT PHILADELPHIA: MR. RICHARD HENRY LEE READING THE ORIGINAL DOCUMENT OF THE DECLARATION OF INDEPENDENCE.

They heard the **Declaration** of Independence.

The Declaration brought freedom to the United States.

The bell was rung for important **events.** Now it has a crack!

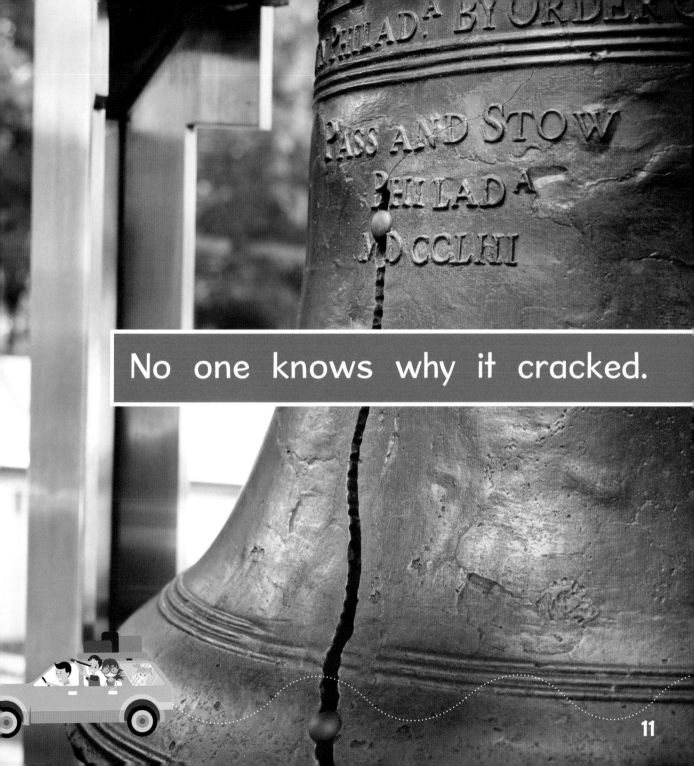

No one knows why it cracked.

The bell doesn't ring anymore. But many people **visit** it.

Did you find these words?

They heard the **Declaration** of Independence.

The bell was rung for important **events**.

It is a symbol of **independence**.

But many people **visit** it.

Photo Glossary

 **declaration** (dek-luh-RAY-shuhn): An announcement of something important.

 **events** (i-VENTS): Interesting or important activities or celebrations.

 **independence** (in-di-PEN-duhns): Freedom, or the state of being independent.

 **visit** (VIZ-it): To go somewhere and spend time with people or exploring a place.

Index

About the Author

K.A. Robertson is a writer and editor who enjoys learning about the history of the United States. She has visited the Liberty Bell many times!

www.rourkeeducationalmedia.com

PHOTO CREDITS: Cover: ©LoudRedCreative; p2,8,14,15: ©Library of Congress; p2,10,14,15: ©Bastiaan Slabbers; p2,6,14,15: ©Krapels; p2,13,14,15: ©Aleksander Mirski; p3: ©RomoloTavani; p4: ©f11photo; p7: ©DBTulac; p8,9: ©DNY59; p11: ©Library of Congress

Edited by: Keli Sipperley
Cover and interior design by: Kathy Walsh

Library of Congress PCN Data
Liberty Bell / K.A. Robertson
(Visiting U.S. Symbols)
ISBN 978-1-64369-059-9 (hard cover)(alk. paper)
ISBN 978-1-64369-080-3 (soft cover)
ISBN 978-1-64369-206-7 (e-Book)
Library of Congress Control Number: 2018955829

Printed in the United States of America, North Mankato, Minnesota